OHIO

A PICTURE MEMORY

Text
Bill Harris

Captions
Roger W. Hicks

Design
Teddy Hartshorn

Photography
Colour Library Books Ltd.
FPG International

Picture Researcher
Leora Kahn

Commissioning Editor
Andrew Preston

Editorial
David Gibbon

Director of Production
Gerald Hughes

CLB 2859
This 1992 editon published by Crescent Books,
distributed by Outlet Books, Inc., a Random House Company,
40 Engelhard Avenue, Avenel, New Jersey 07001.
Color separations by Scantrans (PTE) Ltd., Singapore
Printed and bound in Singapore
ISBN 0 517 07263 7
8 7 6 5 4 3 2 1

OHIO

A PICTURE MEMORY

CRESCENT BOOKS
NEW YORK · AVENEL, NEW JERSEY

Hardly a month goes by when we don't read of some new study that says American schoolchildren don't have the vaguest notion of such things as where South America is or whether Vietnam is in Asia or Africa. But if our kids are growing up to be geographical illiterates, a lot of grown-ups have a problem, too, at least as far as Ohio is concerned. In New York and New England, they say it's the heart of the Midwest, and Californians place it somewhere "back East." Of course, some Californians consider Iowa an Eastern State, too, and many of them aren't quite sure it isn't just an alternate spelling of Ohio. Most demographers classify Ohio as a Great Lakes State because most of its northern border is on Lake Erie, but so is New York's northern boundary, and the whole southern shore of Lake Ontario is in New York. The northwest corner of Pennsylvania is on Lake Erie, too, but, like New York, it is part of the "Northeast," which is what many Ohioans say defines their position, too. Is it any wonder the kids are confused?

The problem is confounded for them in history class. The Founding Fathers officially called the region north and west of the Ohio River the Northwest Territory, and its first white settlers were Virginians who considered it a natural extension of their southern colony. A bit further north, other Ohio settlers were governed by the Connecticut Legislature, which called a corner of the territory its "Western Reserve" almost until Ohio became a state in 1803. But if no one makes the mistake of listing Ohio among the New England States, there are dozens of towns there that outdo Massachusetts in terms of New England charm, and the people who established Ohio's first major town arrived aboard a ship called the *Mayflower*!

The region was first explored by the French, who claimed it as their own until the British took it away from them after the French and Indian War. Twenty years later, in 1783, they were forced to hand it over to the Americans in the treaty that ended the Revolutionary War. The Continental Congress considered the new Northwest Territory its great hope for raising money to cover the country's war debt, but when it tried to auction the land there weren't many takers. The English, it turned out, were having second thoughts about the prize they had lost and were working with their former Indian allies to keep potential settlers at bay. Congress, meanwhile, had enough problems and decided to turn this one over to what modern lawmakers call "the private sector." It was only natural that they'd turn to New England, because that's where the best salesmen were. Among them was General Rufus Putnam, a hero of the late war and a good friend of George Washington, who put the icing on the salesman's cake by welcoming their new community into the family with the words: "No colony in America was ever settled under such favorable auspices."

General Putnam and his Boston friends had incorporated themselves into an enterprise called the Ohio Company, and they negotiated with the government for a million-and-a-half acres of land around the point where the Muskingum River joins the Ohio. About three-quarters of its shareholders were war veterans who were entitled to free farms as a reward for faithful service, but if they were short on funds, they were tough enough to tame the frontier, and there was money enough in the company to help them get started. Among their expenses was building the great fortified ship *Mayflower*, which carried forty-eight of them down the Ohio River one spring day in 1788. According to Putnam's diary, the trip was "uneventful," and that may be why they sailed right past the mouth of the Muskingum. Fortunately, there was a wilderness fort a little further along and soldiers and pioneers put their backs to it and towed the boat to the site of Ohio's first settlement.

They might have named the place for one of the towns they left behind as their New England ancestors had, but all the available names reminded them of the despised British, and they voted instead to honor Marie Antoinette, the Queen of France, for her support in the war, and they called it Marietta. It was a rather frilly name for a fortified town that was a series of connected blockhouses surrounded by a high wooden wall, but they all believed that some day it would as pretty a place as any town in Massachusetts. General Putnam had already ordered the plans, in fact. He had also sent word back to Massachusetts that the Ohio Company was a going concern, and hundreds loaded their belongings into covered wagons carrying huge signs that proclaimed they were headed "To Marietta on The Ohio."

But the Ohio Company wasn't without competition. Two years after the founding of Marietta, John Cleves Symmes, a New Jersey Congressman turned land speculator, sold a huge tract along the Ohio River to another group of speculators who planted a town that became known as Cincinnati in honor of the society of retired Revolutionary War officers. A few years later he sold 60,000 acres at the meeting point of the Mad and Stillwater rivers, and a half-dozen men and their families started building a town named for one of them, Jonathan Dayton.

But Judge Symmes wasn't quite on the up and up. He contracted with Congress to buy a million acres of the Northwest Territory, but never managed to raise the money to pay for it. That didn't stop him from selling it, though, and he also sold thousands of acres that weren't included in his contract. Eventually Congress took the land back, creating a legal tangle it's amazing isn't still going through the courts. Most buyers, some two or three times removed from the Symmes Company, were able to make deals with the Government and kept their land. But Symmes himself lost every penny he had earned, most of it to lawyers. It was hard to find anyone in the Territory who felt sorry for him, but if his operation was a bit shady, he had done more than even General Putnam to convince Americans that they had a future west of the Allegheny Mountains.

And there were other promoters out there who took their campaign abroad, where they touted Ohio as "the garden of the universe." Nothing wrong with that, of course, but these entrepreneurs said they owned the place and they didn't. The prime perpetrator was William Duer, a Treasury Department official, who made a secret deal with the partners of the Ohio Company to make a small down payment on five million acres. Unaware of

Duer's involvement, Congress approved the option, which he used to make himself a silent partner in a new operation called the Scioto Company. Duer's plan was to sell the land in Europe, where no one would question the deeds he had printed, and then use the proceeds to make the deeds legal. His star salesman was Joel Barlow, a Connecticut lawyer with all the instincts of a Yankee peddler. In a matter of weeks, Barlow sold one hundred thousand acres to buyers in Paris, France, and the proud new owners of a piece of Ohio began packing their bags.

The deal Barlow offered promised his French customers that Scioto would pay for their passage to America in return for a contract that they would work for the company for three years. As a bonus for such service, they would also be entitled to a house and fifty acres of land. And if they signed right away, Barlow said, his company had authorized him to give them a free cow. In spite of the come-on, his first five hundred customers weren't farmers, but city people who made their living at such trades as watchmaking, glass blowing and wood carving. That was probably because the salesman told them that the town he was selling was already thriving, and that the countryside for miles around was settled with people who would probably be happy to have their watches kept in repair and would pay handsomely for a delicately carved mantle over their fireplace.

The French contingent set sail for Alexandria, Virginia, because Mr. Barlow had told them that, although Ohio was only about thirty miles from the coast, it was easier to get there by boat now that the Potomac and Ohio Rivers were connected by a canal. The canal didn't exist, of course, but that was a moot point. The town they were headed for didn't exist, either. Worse, as they discovered as soon as they landed, the Scioto Company didn't own any land in the Ohio Territory and neither did they. But their luck hadn't completely run out.

It was only natural that President Washington would hear that there were five hundred disillusioned Frenchmen in his home town and, possibly remembering how the French had come to his rescue at Yorktown, he arranged to have the Scioto options turned over to the Ohio Company. Then he sent a message to his friend, General Putnam, to start building a town for the new immigrants.

Putnam's men worked all summer building eighty log cabins arranged in neat rows of twenty each, surrounding them with a palisade that had a strong blockhouse at each corner. It was a far cry from Paris, but in mid-October,1790, the new town of Gallipolis came to life. They managed to make it through the winter with food supplied by Putnam's hunters, and in the spring men who had never touched a hoe in all their lives began planting crops. A few of them had brought gardening books along, but no survival guides, and what they chose to plant were things like asparagus and artichokes, grapes and olives. But they muddled through for several years before they discovered that they had a new problem. Congress eventually gave them 24,000 acres of land, but General Putnam had built their town on land belonging to his company, which expected to be paid for it. Most of the French settlers responded by drifting away, and within a few years the place they had hopefully called the "City of Gauls" was taken over by distinctly Anglo-Saxon squatters, and it eventually grew into a thriving river town, about as "typically American" as any town in America.

"Typically American" is a description that perfectly suits any number of Ohio towns. It was the first part of America to have been settled by families born and raised on this side of the Atlantic. All kinds of people were drawn to the Northwest Territory when it was opened for settlement; some were rich and some were not, some were deeply religious, others were trying to escape the hard-nosed rule of the New England churches. They moved west from the Middle Atlantic States, too, and farmers from Georgia and the Carolinas crossed the Ohio to mingle with Virginians who were already there. But the majority of the early settlers were from Connecticut. The event that sent thousands of them in the direction of Ohio was the eruption of the Tambora volcano on the Indonesian island of Sumbawa in 1815.

The cloud of ash and debris caused by the eruption hit the American Northeast the following spring, blocking out the sun for months. Snow fell in New England all summer long, ponds were frozen in August and hard frosts ruined every farmer's crops in what they called "the year without a summer." Connecticut was hardest hit, and whole communities uprooted themselves to relocate in "yonder Ohio." More often than not they took their roots along with them, and the towns they established not only looked like the ones they left behind, but were given names like Trumbull and Norwalk, Bridgeport and Greenwich.

The New Englanders also brought missionaries with them to tame the wild frontiersmen who were moving in from Kentucky and Tennessee, but they clearly had their work cut out for them. One of them complained that the Southerners among them "bid fair to grow into a hardened and corrupt society." Whether because of churchmen like him or in spite of them, the prediction proved to be off the mark, but there was no denying that not all Ohio pioneers were cut from the same cloth.

Most of the Southerners who migrated into Ohio had grown up on small farms and had no taste for living in the communities New Englanders preferred. Although they were religious in their own way, they didn't feel the same tug of Manifest Destiny that drove the New Englanders. And, though many of them had fought in the Revolution, they had a deep distrust of all governments, even the one they helped create. All they wanted was a productive piece of land and the chance to live their own lives in their own way. We call them rugged individualists. It was only natural that the New Englanders would call them immoral and lazy. And it was just as natural that, in turn, they would consider the Yankees a bunch of cheating capitalists who not only lusted after their land but were determined to take away all their rights, from making it a crime to get drunk on Sundays to forcing their kids to go to school on weekdays.

But somehow they managed to get along in spite of their differences, and over time Ohioans managed to combine the best of both cultures into something brand new. It even showed in the language. The spare New England accents merged with the softer Southern speech patterns and became an unmistakable dialect we call Midwestern. But there were other influences, too. By mid-century there were as many foreign-born Ohioans as there were Southerners in the 17th state to join the Union, and more had come from homes in Germany and Ireland than had emigrated from Massachusetts or Connecticut. Everyone was welcome, and promoters of Ohio settlement made it a point to tell their potential customers that the only warning they had to offer was that Ohio was no place for anyone "so strongly imbued with the peculiar manners, notions and ways of thought [of their original home] as to be unable to shake them off."

And it wasn't just rhetoric. In those early days, when men were proud to be in control of their own fate in a place where "kin don't count a cuss," everyone considered themselves self-sufficient. But they relied on one another, too. Anyone who need help could usually count on getting it, and sometimes they got help before they knew they needed it. Sometimes it came from an odd little man who seemed to be everywhere at once and usually vanished without waiting for thanks for the good he left behind. He was almost too good to be true, but if he has been relegated to American mythology, Johnny Appleseed was quite real and one of the best things that could have happened to Ohio.

By the time he died in the mid 1830s, John Chapman had wandered west into Indiana, and his short obituary in the Fort Wayne paper said that "he followed the occupation of nursery-man." But remembering Johnny Appleseed as a nursery man is almost the same as recalling George Washington as a planter.

Chapman wandered through the wilderness west of Pittsburgh for more than fifty years planting apple trees as well as medicinal plants he knew would be useful to the settlers who would follow in his footsteps. But even before he reached Pittsburgh, he had planted orchards all the way from Massachusetts.

Everyone who knew him loved him. Even the Indians, who were suspicious of all white men, made an exception in Johnny's case. But even those who loved him most had to admit he cut quite a bizarre figure. They say that he wore a shirt made from a coffee sack with holes cut out for his arms, and that a stewing kettle passed for a hat. He never wore shoes, not even in the dead of winter, and he walked everywhere he went, finding his way without the help of a compass.

Deeply religious, Chapman led an utterly selfless life. He didn't own a gun and couldn't hurt a living thing. One of the legends about him says that he didn't build campfires because he didn't want mosquitoes and other insects to be burned to death in the flames. He never ate meat and, if the stories are true, the animals he encountered seemed to understand that he was their friend. One pioneer swore he once saw Johnny playing with a family of bear cubs while their mother looked on benignly. Others remembered that he would never accept a thing from anyone unless he could exchange it for a handful of seeds or a small tree.

No one knew where he'd turn up next. He would just appear at cabin doors around sunset and ask for a place to sleep, but he always refused to lie anywhere but on the floor, and by the time the sun came up in the morning he had vanished as silently as he had appeared, leaving nothing behind but a gift of seeds. But of all the gifts Johnny Appleseed left behind in Ohio, the most impressive was a new lease on life for the city of Mansfield.

The settlement was nothing more than a handful of cabins when an Indian raiding party surrounded it during the War of 1812, and it seemed doomed until Johnny ran thirty miles to the nearest fort and came back with a contingent of soldiers in less than twenty-four hours. The soldiers not only sent the Indians packing, but stayed on to help clear fifty acres and build a fortified town. True to form, Johnny Appleseed silently moved on. Ohio was getting too crowded for him. There were more than a million people spread out between the Ohio River and Lake Erie by then, and more were arriving every day.

Facing page: the Owens-Illinois Building on the banks of the Maumee River, in Toledo. The building's glass-clad walls bring to mind one of the names by which the city is known: "The Glass Capital of the World." Every kind of glass is made here, from the windows of skyscrapers to high-tech optical fibers, from television tubes to automobile windshields.

The Maumee River around which Toledo (overleaf), the eleventh-largest port in the United States, has grown up, is alive with traffic (facing page). The port gives its name to the big new shopping complex in the heart of the city, Portside (above, below, and bottom right). The Lucas County Building (right) bespeaks an older, but no less prosperous Toledo, while Toledo Bridge (top right) is a figurative link with the past. Overleaf: downtown Toledo, seen from the Maumee River.

Portside shopping-and-restaurant complex (these pages and overleaf) is a place to shop, to walk, to relax, to see and be seen. The colorful, modern complex contains a wide variety of shops and restaurants – mostly small, owner-operated businesses that bear little resemblance to the bland, uniform shops that are so often encountered today. Parks, pools, and footpaths bring back the scale and intimacy of an old-fashioned town square, while remaining up-to-the-minute in concept and execution.

President Rutherford B. Hayes lived at Spiegel Grove in Fremont (facing page top), and you can still see the rooms where he lived and worked, including the library (top left), the small parlor (left), and the spacious drawing room (bottom left). Quite different is Cedar Point, Sandusky (above), which has been described as Ohio's best-known fun spot; though it has plenty of rivals to tempt the recreation-seeker, such as Vermilion (below) and the marina at the mouth of the Rocky River (facing page bottom).

Cleveland (these pages and overleaf) is, like so much of Ohio, a blend of old and new. "The Mall" (above) is a handsome open space in the middle of the city, while the Old Stone Church (below) is exactly what its name suggests. The Sohio Building (facing page) is a reminder of Cleveland's commercial acumen and the Museum of Art (right), one of the finest museums in the country, a reflection of its wealth. Bottom right: the fountains outside the Convention Center. Top right: Cuyahoga County Soldiers' and Sailors' Monument.

The magnificent glass-roofed Cleveland Arcade, in downtown Cleveland (below) is said to have been the first indoor shopping complex in the United States. It was built in 1890 and is one of the finest enclosed shopping areas in the world, combining traditional elegance and the finest of modern shops and restaurants. Its graceful proportions and superb detailing impress even the most sophisticated of world travelers. The Terminal Tower (facing page) is one of the best-known landmarks of the city, especially at night when its floodlit majesty dominates the skyline.

Cleveland Metroparks (facing page), only twenty miles east of Cleveland, are sylvan relief from the pressures and pleasures of the city. There are twelve major parks, totaling 16,000 acres, around Cleveland. The Hale Farm and Village (this page), located in Cuyahoga Valley National Recreation Area, is a "Living History" village, where old and reconstructed buildings re-create a mid-19th century Ohio village. Overleaf: Lawnfield, at Mentor, the last home of President Garfield.

For sports fans there is the Pro-Football Hall of Fame in Canton (above and top left), and for history buffs Ohio's many restored and re-created villages such as the "Ghost Town" in Findlay (left and bottom left); Ohio Village at Columbus (below), one of some 50 historical sites operated by the Ohio Historical Society; and Roscoe Village at Coshocton (facing page top). There are also historic mills, like the Indian Mill (facing page bottom) on the Sandusky river, and houses like that of President Warren G. Harding at Marion (overleaf).

31

The Avery-Downer House in Granville (facing page) was built in 1842 and is a fine example of Greek Revival architecture. Now the Robbins Hunter Museum, it contains fourteen furnished rooms open to the public. The reception hall (above) was equally suitable for greeting welcome guests, or ignoring unwelcome ones; there were separate parlors for the gentlemen (below) and the ladies (right), and an elegant sideboard and a grandfather clock graced the dining room (top right and bottom right).

Some state capitals were chosen for their very obscurity when rival big cities fought over where the seat of government should be. Columbus (these pages and overleaf), which replaced Chillicothe as the state capital in 1816, thirteen years after Ohio achieved statehood, is not like that. The city is, and has always been, more than just a seat of bureaucrats: its commercial side grew alongside its administrative importance. Today it furnishes the headquarters for a number of major corporations as well as being noted for science and banking. The State Capitol (facing page and right) reflects the city's cosmopolitan origins. Below: a view of the city skyline from the Scioto River.

Dayton is inseparably associated with the history of flight. Hawthorn Hill (below) was the Wright Brothers' home; it is now owned by NCR, the electronics and cash-register company. Also at Dayton is the United States Air Force Museum, where you can see many of the Wrights' instruments, blueprints, and a scrap of fabric from the wing of the very first heavier-than-air flyer, the 1903 Kitty Hawk. Exhibits also include "war birds," from the original wood-and-wire models to the latest supersonic aircraft, via a Boeing P-12 and World War Two bombers like the B24.

41

The styles of architecture in Cincinnati, "Queen of the West," are diverse, ranging from the neo-classical Hyde Park Medical Arts Building (below) through the Proctor and Gamble Building (top left) and the Riverfront Stadium (facing page top) to the modern Convention Center (bottom left). The Tyler Davis Memorial Fountain (above) is the centerpiece of Fountain Square (left), while the skyline (facing page bottom) is varied and exciting. Overleaf: the Cincinnati skyline, seen from the Kentucky side of the Ohio River.

Cincinnati's Riverfront Stadium (below and overleaf), home of the Reds, dominates almost any view from the river. The Ohio River – the "O-he-yo" or "Great River" of the Iroquois – shares with the Mississippi such magnificent riverboats as the Delta Queen (facing page top). The river is now spanned at Cincinnati by six bridges, including the Central Bridge (facing page bottom). Among many impressive buildings in the downtown area (facing page center) are the Central Trust Building on the left, and the Arens Building on the right.

The Suspension Bridge (facing page top), crossing the Ohio River, was designed by John Roebling and built in 1868. Central Bridge (facing page bottom) is owned by the State of Tennessee; the Suspension Bridge, and the C.W. Bailey Bridge, can be seen behind it. The bronze figures of the Tyler Davidson Memorial Fountain (below) were cast in Munich – an indication of Cincinnati's strong historical links with Germany. The fountain was given to the city in 1871 by Henry Probasco.

There is plenty to see and do around Cincinnati, but the Seven Caves region (facing page) is surely one of the most magical places, rich in legend and history, as well as in ecological and geological interest. The appeal of King's Island, an amusement park (below and bottom left) is quite different, while Cincinnati Zoo (above) was one of the first zoos to use barless enclosures to allow visitors to see animals in a park-like setting. It is the second-oldest zoo in the country. Fork Lake Park (left and top left) is a "Living History" village.

Adena (below), a 22-room Georgian mansion made from local sandstone, was built in 1807, for Thomas Worthington, one of the earliest governors of Ohio. The house is now open to the public, and many rooms, including the elegant parlor (right) and the dining room (center right), and the sternly functional kitchen (bottom right), have now been restored to the way they would have looked in the early nineteenth century. From the lawn of Adena you can see Mount Logan, just as it appears on the State Seal.

Reminders of a rural age are everywhere outside the big cities – and often, not so far outside. In western Ohio, just off Highway 180, rich cornfields ripple in the breeze (facing page top). Near Cincinnati, aromatic tobacco cures in a traditional red-painted barn (below). An old, hand-painted advertisement on a barn near Athens urges the passer-by to chew Mail Pouch tobacco (above), while the other farms on these pages can be seen near Chillicothe (left); at Somerset (facing page bottom); near Marietta (bottom left) and off Highway 180 (top left).

Ohio abounds in state parks, often strategically sited near major cities. Burr Oak State Park (below, and facing page bottom), near Athens, offers beautiful woods, and tranquil lakes as well as swimming, fishing, boat rentals and more. Shawnee State Forest (facing page top), outside Portsmouth, is the largest in Ohio and several state parks exist within its boundaries. Overleaf: Salt Fork State Park, near Cambridge, is cool and mysterious in an early-morning mist. Recreational possibilities in its 20,000-plus acres include hiking, swimming, boating, fishing, and hunting.